100 SONGS

GN00889007

Family Worship

Enabling generations

to worship and

celebrate

together

foreword by
Graham Kendrick

We hope you enjoy *Family Worship*. Further copies are
available from your local Kevin Mayhew stockist.

In case of difficulty, or to request a catalogue,
please contact the publisher direct by writing to:

The Sales Department
world wide worship
Buxhall
Stowmarket
Suffolk IP14 3BW

Phone 01449 737978
Fax 01449 737834
E-mail info@kevinmayhewltd.com

First published in Great Britain in 2002 by world wide worship.

© Copyright 2002 world wide worship.

ISBN 1 84003 904 3
ISMN M 57024 035 7
Catalogue No: 1400323

0 1 2 3 4 5 6 7 8 9

Cover design by Angela Selfe

Music setter: Donald Thomson
Proof reader: Sally Gough

Printed and bound in Great Britain

Important Copyright Information

The Publishers wish to express their gratitude to the copyright owners who have granted permission to include their copyright material in this book. Full details are indicated on the respective pages.

The **words** of most of the songs in this publication are covered by a **Church Copyright Licence** which is available from Christian Copyright Licensing International. This allows local church reproduction on overhead projector acetates, in service bulletins, songsheets, audio/visual recording and other formats.

The **music** in this book is covered by the additional **Music Reproduction Licence** which is issued by CCLI in the territories of Europe and Australasia. You may photocopy the music and words of the songs in the book provided:

> You hold a current Music Reproduction Licence from CCLI.

> The copyright owner of the song you intend to photocopy is included in the Authorised Catalogue List which comes with your Music Reproduction Licence.

The Music Reproduction Licence is **not** currently available in the USA or Canada.

Full details of CCLI can be obtained from their Web site (www.ccli.com) or you can contact them direct at the following offices:

Christian Copyright Licensing (Europe) Ltd
PO Box 1339, Eastbourne, East Sussex, BN21 1AD, UK
Tel: +44 (0)1323 417711; Fax: +44 (0)1323 417722; E-mail: info@ccli.co.uk

CCL Asia-Pacific Pty Ltd (Australia and New Zealand)
PO Box 6644, Baulkham Hills Business Centre, NSW 2153, Australia
Tel: +61 (02) 9894-5386; Toll Free Phone: 1-800-635-474
Fax: +61 (02) 9894-5701; Toll Free Fax: 1-800-244-477
E-mail executive@ccli.co.au

Christian Copyright Licensing Inc
17201 NE Sacramento Street, Portland, Oregon 97230, USA
Tel: +1 (503) 257 2230; Toll Free Phone: 1 (800) 234 2446;
Fax: +1 (503) 257 2244; E-mail executive@ccli.com

Please note, all texts and music in this book are protected by copyright and if you do not possess a licence from CCLI they may not be reproduced in any way for sale or private use without the consent of the copyright owner.

Foreword

The challenge of leading worship when all ages are present is one which can daunt many service and worship leaders! The old adage that 'you can't please all of the people all of the time' can sometimes seem far too appropriate for all-age services. Do you use 'children's songs' at the risk of patronising the youth; do you use 'youth songs' at the risk of alienating the adults; do you use 'adult songs' at the risk of failing to engage the children and youth?

Where the *Family Worship* collection of songs really comes into its own is in the provision of a broad range of material that crosses the (artificial) boundaries that can be perceived to exist between worship for adults, children and youth. The songs have lyrics that are accessible to children, yet acceptable to adults, and they have a depth and weight that is sometimes lacking in the 'lighter' type of songs that sometimes tend to be used in all-age services. The musical styles are very varied, and it is this variety that gives the collection its strength – in using a selection of the songs in any one service, you will go a long way to ensuring that there really is something for everyone.

I have known Mike Burn for many years, and have watched as he has developed, not only in his own writing, but also in encouraging other writers from a grass roots level in our own church, Ichthus Christian Fellowship, and from other churches, to write songs that will serve the church in worship. I have no hesitation in warmly recommending this collection of songs to you.

GRAHAM KENDRICK

Introduction

Do you sometimes dread all-age services? I know I do...

The origins of this songbook stretch back 10 years or so, to the early nineties. As a worship leader then, I could choose from a huge range of material, songs old and new, that would fit pretty much every need in the services that I was involved in – except for one: the 'children's slot'. I used to struggle to find songs that I was happy to use – sure, there were plenty of children's songs available, many with actions, but somehow they didn't quite seem to flow with the rest of the worship. In fact, I would often be keen for the slot to be over, and the children could go out to their Sunday School, so that we could get on with some 'proper worship'. The thought that the whole church should be able to worship effectively with all ages together really hadn't crossed my mind then, such was the level of my sensitivity!

At that time, in observing my own growing children in worship, however, I began to realise that much of what we were doing in the worship time while all ages were present was largely inaccessible to them. A fairly common answer to the question 'Did you enjoy the service today?' would yield the dreaded answer 'No, it was boring!' Take the same children on their own, in a different context, however, and they clearly loved to worship, so it wasn't a lack of willingness on their part to engage in worship, it was the approach and structure, and in part the choice of songs, in our services that was in question.

So I began to look for songs that could be used while the children were in, which would help them to participate, without being patronising or simplistic for the adults. I soon discovered that songs that could fit that category were few and far between – they did exist, but it took a lot of searching, and trial and error to find them. The pastor of my church at the time recognised the problem too, and suggested that I try to write some songs that would fit the need. In trying to do that, and in working with other writers that I knew, we collected enough songs to record an album, and so *Family Worship 1 – Let Praise Break Out* was released. Considering that the album was recorded on a shoe-string budget, and with most of the songs being debut songs from the various writers, we were astonished at the positive response that it received from many different churches around the UK and worldwide, and realised that the nature of the songs was filling a definite gap.

One song in particular from that first album, 'I reach up high' by Judy Bailey, has been used far and wide, and perhaps typifies the 'Family

Worship genre' (if such a thing could or should exist!) The song works at all sorts of levels – it is an action song that children love, it has simple yet profound lyrics in the verse that work at many different levels, and it is strong musically. Other songs from that first album, like 'I'm singing your praise' and 'God, you can use me', have been very popular, not only in churches but also schools, which was a spin-off benefit that we had not envisaged.

There was one criticism, however, from a number of people who gave us feedback on that first album, and it was this: whilst the album had plenty of songs that could be used very effectively to engage children and adults in worship together, it didn't really have any songs that were appealing to teenagers and young adults, and so the album didn't quite fulfil the promise of all-age worship, excluding to an extent, as it did, the youth.

When we were ready to record *Family Worship 2 – With One Voice*, we felt we had addressed this criticism and included a very strong contemporary worship song, 'Waterfall', which had come from a youth-orientated church in Ichthus, the 'Brown Bear', and since then 'Brown Bear Music' (Ian Mizen & Andy Pressdee) have written many more worship songs that are received enthusiastically by youth, but are equally at home in an all-age service, and several of those songs appear in this collection.

The third and fourth Family Worship albums, *Fire and Rain* and *Rising Generation*, again included songs that were accessible to children, youth and adults, and we felt that the concept was maturing to the point that a compilation songbook would be warranted. So here it is, and in addition to all of the songs to date from the Family Worship albums, there are over 40 additional songs, many of them previously unpublished, which cover a wide variety of writers, styles and subjects, but all have the common thread that links together all of the songs in this book: they are ideal for use on a Sunday morning or at other times when all ages are in worship together.

I do hope that this book is a useful addition to the material available for your worship services, and pray that God will use the songs to draw the whole of HIS family together in worship.

MIKE BURN
Family Worship Resources, London, 2002
www.familyworship.org.uk

1 All the world can offer
(Because)

Words and Music: Colin Hardy
arr. Dave Bankhead

1. All the world can of - fer,   none of it com-
2. All the world's wis -dom,   chose to cru - ci-

pares with you.   All the gold and sil - ver
fy the truth.   But when you called I fol -lowed,

can't re -place the God I love.   All the world sees
I have giv - en ev - 'ry-thing for you.   Je - sus, my

pre-cious,   one day it will fade a -way,
trea-sure,   you are my heart's de - sire.

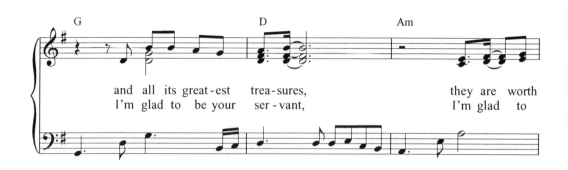

and all its great-est trea-sures,　　　　they are worth
I'm glad to be your ser-vant,　　　　I'm glad to

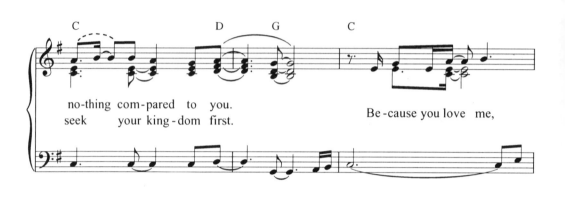

no-thing com-pared to you.　　Be-cause you love me,
seek your king-dom first.

be-cause you called me,

be-cause you saved me I'm not liv-ing for this world,

D C G   *Chorus*

'cause I'm liv-ing for you. Don't know   what I'd

G/B D   C

do with-out your love, don't know what I'd do with-out you;

G   G/B D

don't know what I'd do with-out your love, your love is the

C   1. G   2. G

on - ly ans - wer. Don't know what I'd

2 A rainfall in drought

(By your wounds)

Words and Music: Anju Ebanks

Family Worship

3 A time to mourn

Words and Music: Mike Burn

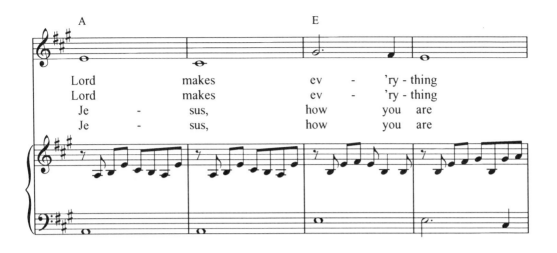

Lord   makes   ev - 'ry - thing
Lord   makes   ev - 'ry - thing
Je - sus,   how   you   are
Je - sus,   how   you   are

beau - ti-ful   in   its   time.   A time for
beau - ti-ful
beau - ti-ful   to   my   eyes.   A time for
beau - ti-ful

in   its   time.   Though the grass   will
to   my   eyes.   Though the grass   will

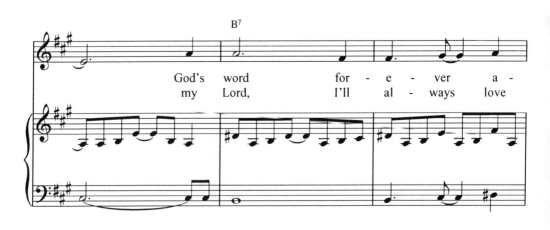

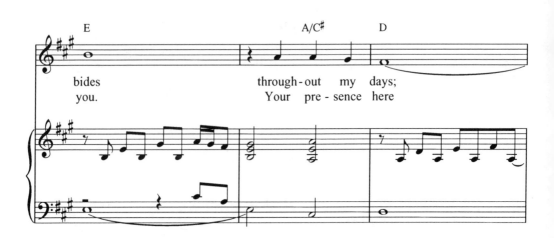

C#   F#m

in all I say or do, may the
is more than life to me; to be

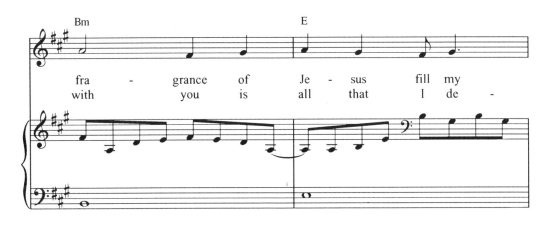

Bm   E

fra - grance of Je - sus fill my
with   you is all that I de -

A   **1.**   **2.**

                  D.S.

time.   2. A time to
sire.

4 Be joyful

Words and Music: Mike Burn

Be joy-ful in hope, pa-tient in your trou- -bles, and faith - ful in prayer.

Be faith - ful in prayer. Ro-mans twelve, verse twelve says be

faith - ful in prayer, Ro-mans twelve, verse twelve

says be faith - ful in prayer.

5 Calling on the Spirit

Words and Music: Judy Bailey

2. Calling on the Spirit, *(echo)*
   Holy Spirit, *(echo)*
   come to your people, *(echo)*
   we're crying out again. *(echo)*
   Fire on the church, Lord, *(echo)*
   rain on the nations, *(echo)*
   your salvation *(echo)*
   be known throughout the earth.

6 Celebrate Jesus

Words and Music: Ian Booth

Ce-le-brate Je-sus be-cause he is good, his mer-cy for e-ver en-

dures. Ce-le-brate Je-sus be-cause he is good, ce-le-

brate the Lord a-bove all lords.

1. Rais-ing the hum-ble one, heal-ing the bro-ken heart,

2. He is the King of kings,
   reigns over ev'rything,
   he's the Almighty One,
   his love will never end,
   greater than anything,
   celebrate!

7 Christ before me

Words: taken from *St. Patrick's Breastplate*

Music: Mike Burn

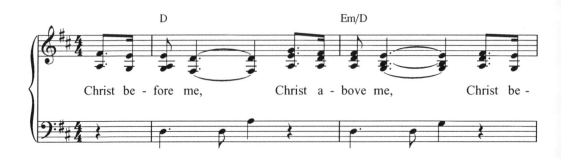

Christ be - fore me, Christ a - bove me, Christ be -

neath me, Christ be - side. Christ my vis - ion, Christ my

wis - dom, Christ my com - fort, Christ my guide.

I bind un - to my self this day the strong and ho - ly

name. Praise to the migh - ty God of my sal-va - tion, three in

one and one in three. I bind un - to my - self this day the strong

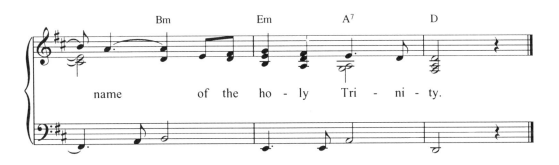

name of the ho - ly Tri - ni - ty.

Family Worship

8 Come and sing

Words and Music: Mike Burn

1. Come and sing, come and sing, come and sing
come and dance, come and dance

to Je - sus now. Come and sing, come and sing,
for Je - sus now. Come and dance, come and dance,

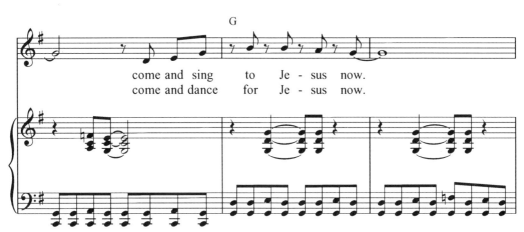

come and sing to Je - sus now.
come and dance for Je - sus now.

Give him thanks for who he is, give him thanks for what
Dance for joy be - fore the throne, let your in - hi - bi-

he's done, come and sing. Je -
- tions go, come and dance.

Chorus

- sus won it all for us when he shed his blood on the cross.

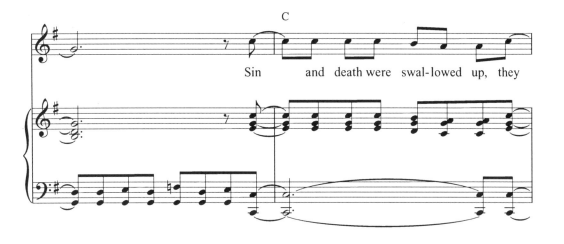

Sin and death were swal-lowed up, they

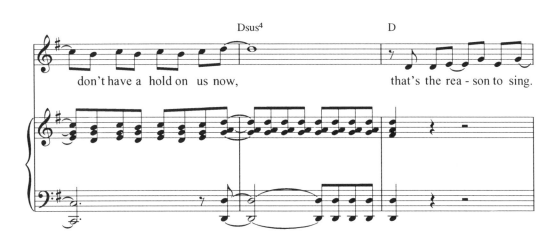

don't have a hold on us now, that's the rea-son to sing.

2. Come and dance,

9 Crossing over

Words and Music: Graeme Young

Swing, with a driving bassline

Chorus

Cros-sing o-ver, leave be-hind the de-sert sand.

Cros-sing o - ver in-to the

life that God has planned. Cros-sing o-

-ver, Je-sus takes us by the hand.

Cros-sing o - ver in-to a new land.

1. We are not go - ing back where we came from, we are not

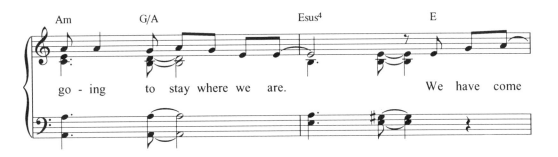

go - ing to stay where we are. We have come

a long way al - rea - dy, now the new land is not far.

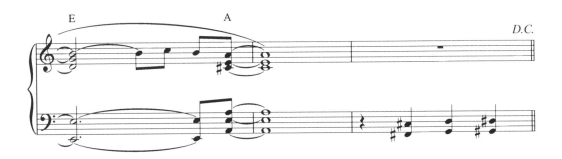

2. We are not going to give way to Satan,
   we are not going to listen to lies,
   he may think that the land is his land,
   but he'll get a big surprise.

3. We are not going to doubt Jesus' pow'r,
   we are not going to turn back in fear,
   the commander of heaven's armies
   is standing with us here.

4. We are not going to visit, then come back,
   we are not going to miss out, no way!
   We have heard of a land of revival
   so we're on the move today.

10 Drawn from every tribe

(Revelation 7)

Words and Music: David Lyle Morris
and Faith Forester

1. Drawn from ev - 'ry tribe, ev - 'ry tongue and na - tion,
2. We are those who fol - low through scenes of fi - ery trial,
3. Ne - ver will we hun - ger, we'll no long - er thirst, there's

ga - thered be - fore the throne.
draw - ing from wells of grace.
shade from the heat of day.

Cast - ing down their crowns, they fall at his feet and
Through the dark - est val - ley, from the depths of pain, we'll
Led to springs of life, Je - sus our Shep - herd, will

wor - ship the Lord a - lone.
come to that ho - ly place.
wipe ev - 'ry tear a - way.

Our

11 Everywhere I go

(Jesus, my friend)

Words and Music: Katy Trigg

12 Father, I do adore you

Words and Music: Judy Bailey and Dave Bankhead

Flowing

Fa - ther, I do a - dore you, wor - ship be-

fore you, I love you, Lord.

You have o-pened up my eyes to see such beau-ty in your face, a

love that cared e-nough to set me free. And my heart is filled with won-der at the

glo-ry of your grace, I'm so thank-ful, Lord, that now you live in me.

2. Jesus, I do adore you . . .   3. Spirit, I do adore you . . .

13 Father's seeking

(With one voice)

Words and Music: Mike Burn

1. Fa-ther's seek-ing those who'll wor-ship him,
2. Je-sus draws us to the Fa-ther's heart;

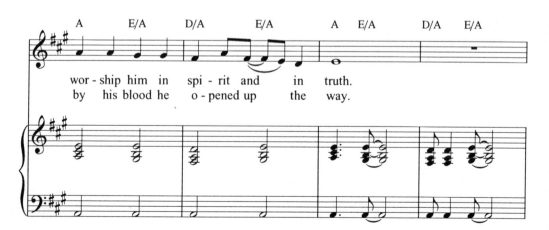

wor-ship him in spi-rit and in truth.
by his blood he o-pened up the way.

14 Fill my life, O Lord my God   *(Praying God)*

Words and Music: Judy Bailey

Fill my life, O Lord my God, in ev - 'ry part with

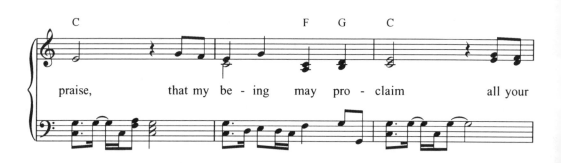

praise, that my be - ing may pro - claim all your

be - ing and your ways. Pray-ing, God be in my head,

in my un - der-stand - ing, Lord. Pray-ing, God be in my eyes,

15 Fly free

(Song for Wales)

Words and Music: Mike Burn

Chorus

Fly free, Spi-rit of God, fly free, free as a dove, draw me up in your flights of love. Show me all that you see, help me to feel what you feel, re - veal the Fa - ther's heart for this land.

Last time

To verses

1. The

Spi - rit of God is brood - ing o - ver this

land, the Spi - rit of God is sing - ing

of the Fa - ther's plans. The Spi - rit of God is wait -

- ing; long - ing for the day when the

Chorus
D.S.

prai-ses of God will ring loud and clear once more. Fly

2. The church of God is stirring
all through this land,
the church of God is praying,
lifting holy hands.
The church of God is rising,
rising to take her place,
joining heav'nly hosts
singing praises to the Lamb.

16 From where the sun rises

Words and Music: Graham Kendrick

Chorus

E-ven in the night when the sun goes down, we're giv-ing you praise;

pas-sing it a-long as the world goes round, we're

giv-ing you praise.

2. We're lift-ing our

2. We're lifting our faces,
    looking at the One we all love –
    we're giving you praise.
    All colours and races
    joining with the angels above –
    we're giving you praise,
    giving you praise.

17 Give, and it shall be given

Words and Music: Mike Burn

1. Give, and it shall be giv - en!

O, you can't out - give the Lord your

God. One thing is cer - tain in the king - dom of

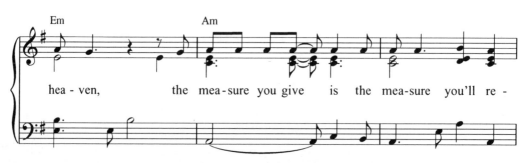

hea - ven, the mea-sure you give is the mea-sure you'll re-

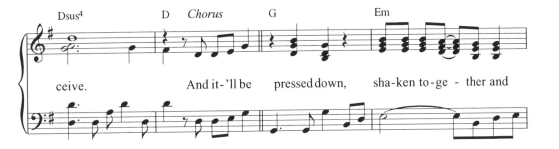

ceive.   And it-'ll be   pressed down,   sha-ken to-ge - ther and

o - ver - flow - ing: it - 'll be   pressed   down,

sha-ken to-ge - ther and   o - ver - flow - ing.

2. Don't rob God of your firstfruits,
   give the most you can and then some more.
   He longs to open a window from heaven
   and pour out a blessing so big you'll be amazed!

3. God's building now his kingdom,
   and his kingdom's rule will never end.
   If you will give him your life, your time, your money,
   you'll store up a treasure no one can steal away.

18 God is our Father *(Kingdom of heaven our goal)*

Words and Music: David Lyle Morris
and Nick Wynne-Jones

2. Look at the lilies
   and see how they grow:
   they are clothed by God's goodness
   in beautiful show.
   Our Father in heaven
   who cares for each flower,
   provides for us always
   so great is his power.

   Bridge 2:
   The kingdom of heaven
   and his righteousness
   we will seek with a passion
   so all may be blessed.

19 God, you can use me

Words and Music: Graeme Young

2. God, you can use me, *(repeat)*
   that the world may see the Lord Jesus,
   God, you can use me.

3. God, you can use me, *(repeat)*
   that the world may love the Lord Jesus,
   God, you can use me.

4. God, you can use us, *(repeat)*
   that the world may praise the Lord Jesus,
   God, you can use us.

20 Grace and love

Words and Music: Mark Harris

Chorus
Grace and love you have shown me,
I will ne-ver be the same. In your love and your for-
give - ness, you took my sin a - way, you took the blame.
O, Je - sus,
O, Je - sus,

how can I love you more?
how can I thank you, Lord?
O,
O,

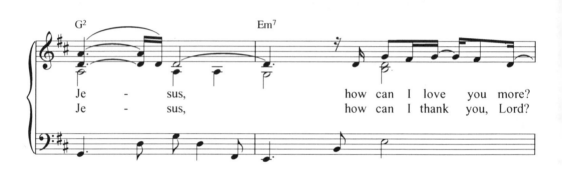

Je - sus, how can I love you more?
Je - sus, how can I thank you, Lord?

Grace and
O,

Je - sus, how can I thank you, Lord?

O, Je - sus, how can I love you more?

O, Je - sus,

how can I e-ver un - der-stand? O,

Je - sus, I love you, Lord.

21 Have you not seen?   *(Fire and rain)*

Words and Music: Mike Burn

Have you not seen, have you not heard? The Lord is pour-ing his Spi-rit out. Have you not seen, have you not heard? The Lord is pour-ing his Spi-rit out to-day. Come, Lord Je - sus, more of you, we cry, o-pen hea - ven, ans-wer with your fire. Fire on the church,

22 Heavenly Father

(Prayer song)

Words and Music: Ian Mizen and Andy Pressdee

Strongly rhythmic

1. Hea-ven-ly Fa - ther, may your ho-ly name be lift - ed

high in all the earth.

Hea-ven-ly Fa - ther, let your king-dom come, and your will be

done in all the earth.

2. Heavenly Father, wash away our sins
   and make us holy in your eyes.
   Heavenly Father, guide our hearts and minds
   and keep us hidden in your love.

23 Here I'm bowed

Words and Music: Audrey Traynor and Lynette Boyland

Here I'm bowed, kneel - ing now, in the still-ness of this

time I long to make you mine. Here I'm bowed, kneel - ing

now, I've o - pened up my heart, sur - rend - ered ev - 'ry

part. 1. I look to you, you give me hope,
2. I give to you all that I am,

I know you'll see me through.
and all the things I do.

And when I need you, Lord, you are there,
And now as I ap-proach your throne,

and if I stum - ble, Lord, you still care.
it's you and I, Lord, we're a - lone.

Here I'm

BRIDGE

And I can come no o - ther way, Lord,

Family Worship

24 Holy Jesus

Words and Music: Ian Mizen and Andy Pressdee
arr. Chris Mitchell

Ho - ly Je - sus, burn your fire
Ho - ly Je - sus, full of grace

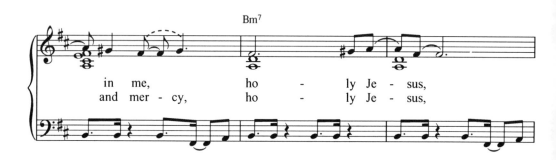

in me, ho - ly Je - sus,
and mer - cy, ho - ly Je - sus,

sanc - ti - fy.
we lift you high.

Son of God,

Word of God, fill me up with your love.

Son of God, Word of God, fill me up with your

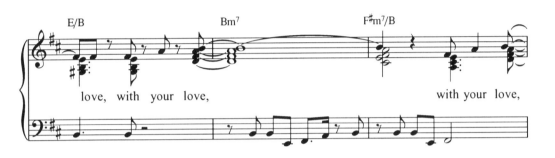

love, with your love, with your love,

with your love,

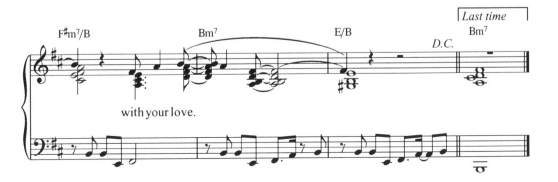

with your love.

25 Hosanna

Words and Music: Ian Booth

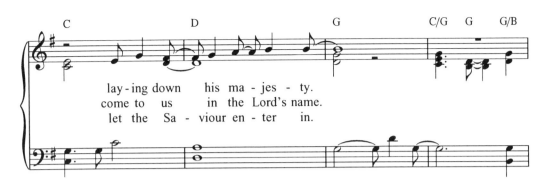

lay - ing down his ma - jes - ty.
come to us in the Lord's name.
let the Sa - viour en - ter in.

He comes to bring to us new life,
Je - sus him - self our on - ly hope,
His love will wipe your tears a - way

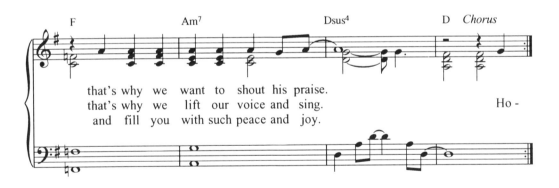

that's why we want to shout his praise.
that's why we lift our voice and sing.
and fill you with such peace and joy.

Ho -

(Final Chorus)

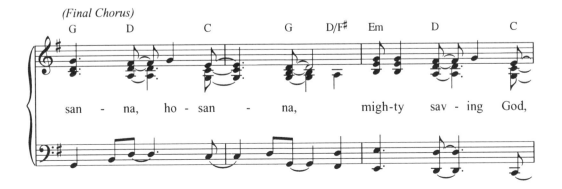

san - na, ho - san - na, migh-ty sav - ing God,

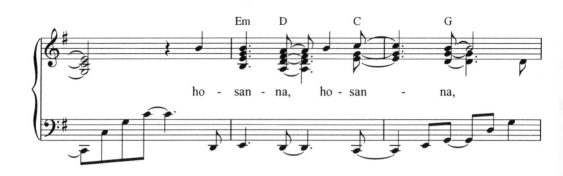

ho - san - na, ho - san - na,

Je - sus, my Lord,

Je - sus, my Lord.

Family Worship

26 I'd reach for the stars

(What can I say?)

Words and Music: Mike Burn

What can I do to show you, Je-sus, that

I love you? I give you my heart,

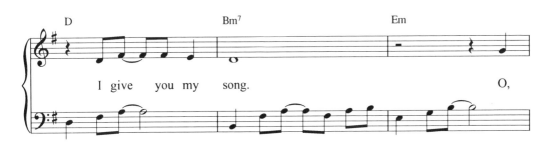

I give you my song. O,

Je-sus, I want you to know. I'd reach for the

2. What do you ask, what should I do?
   Please help me, Jesus, to follow you.
   I give you my life, I give you my will
   O Jesus, I want you to know.

27 I exalt your name

Words and Music: Jo Puleston

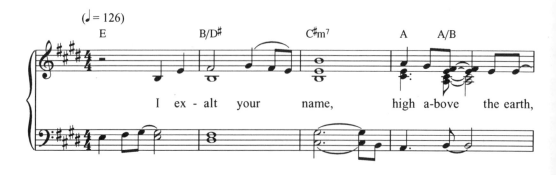

I ex-alt your name, high a-bove the earth,

I now seek your face, Lord, you are the King

and yet my Fa - ther, and I draw close to you.

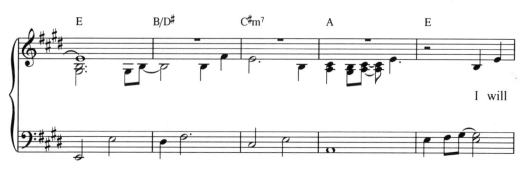

I will

trust your word, and all your pro - mi-ses, leave the

past be-hind, and walk in-to your heart, you are my Fa-

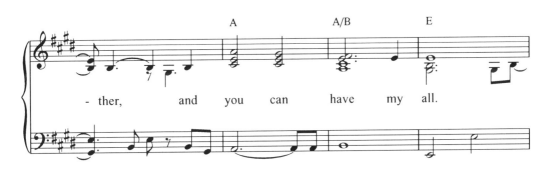

- ther, and you can have my all.

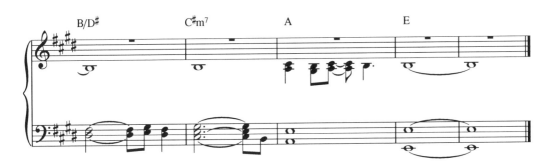

28 If I look in a mirror

Words and Music: Mike Burn

If I look in a mir-ror and there I see my

face, but for-get what I look like as soon as I walk a-way,

that is what it's like if I hear God's

word and I'm fool - ish e-nough not to o - bey.

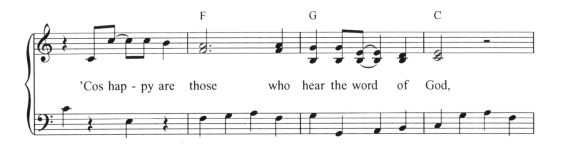

'Cos hap - py are those who hear the word of God,

hap - py are those who trust it and o - bey.

No o - ther way to find true hap - pi - ness than to

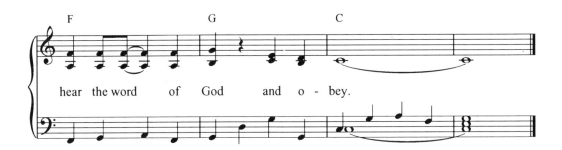

hear the word of God and o - bey.

29 If we admit to God

Words and Music: Kath Fathers

If we ad - mit to God that we've done wrong, (I'm

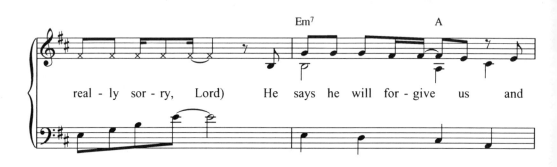

real - ly sor - ry, Lord) He says he will for - give us and

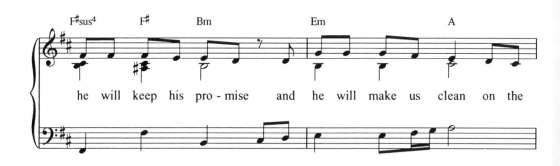

he will keep his pro - mise and he will make us clean on the

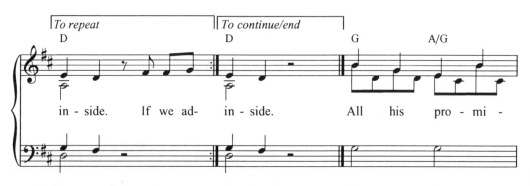

To repeat in - side. If we ad- *To continue/end* in - side. All his pro - mi -

30 If we were to keep quiet

Words and Music: Mike Burn

Joyfully

If we were to keep qui - et, the rocks they would cry out, if

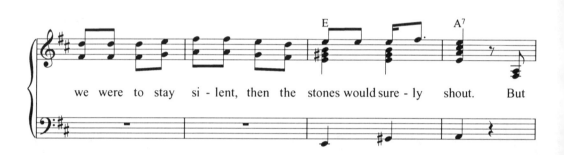

we were to stay si - lent, then the stones would sure - ly shout. But

now we've seen the Lord of lords, we won't keep qui - et a - ny more, be-cause

Je - sus is com - ing soon. Once he came to

die up-on a cross, now he reigns a - live for e-ver -

more. Ho - san - na! Ho - san - na! Ho - san - na in the

high-est heav'n! Je - sus is com - ing soon.

31 If you believe

Words and Music: Mike Burn

If you be-lieve, you will re-ceive what-e-ver you ask for in

prayer. If you be-lieve, you will re-ceive what-

e - ver you ask for in prayer.

Mat-thew twen-ty-one, verse twen-ty-two.

32 If you have faith

Words and Music: Mike Burn

If you have faith as small as a mus-tard seed, you can say to this moun-tain, 'Be thrown in-to the sea!' If you have faith as small as a mus-tard seed, you can say to this moun-tain, 'Be thrown in-to the sea!' I do be-lieve, I do be-lieve, I do be-lieve, Lord, help me o-ver-come my un-be-lief.

33 I love to be with you, Jesus   *(To be with you)*

Words and Music: Mike Burn

34 I'm gonna dance on the streets
(Dance on the streets)

Words and Music: Mike Burn

I'm gon-na dance on the streets,

I'm gon-na sing in the rain .... for the Spi-rit of God

is poured out a-gain.

I'm gon-na shout it a-loud, ... I'm gon-na let the world know

that the ri - ver of God

Je - sus,   Je - sus,

come!   I'm gon - na dance on the streets,

Family Worship

35 I'm putting God's armour on

Words and Music: Mike Burn

I'm put-ting God's ar-mour on, I'm put-ting God's ar-mour on, so I can stand in his might, fight for what is right and walk in the light of the Lord. I'm put-ting God's Lord. Lord. I put on the breast-plate of right-eous-ness, put truth a-round my waist like a belt, I put

36 I'm putting my hand in your hand

Words and Music: Steve Bradshaw

In a laid-back style

I'm put-ting my hand in your hand now, O Je-sus I ask of you

let your Spi-rit flow right through my heart.

I'm put-ting my hand in your hand now, O

Je-sus I ask of you let your Spi-rit flow right through my

heart.   Heal me, Lord,   touch me, Lord,

let your Spi - rit flow   right through my   heart.

Heal me, Lord,   touch me, Lord,

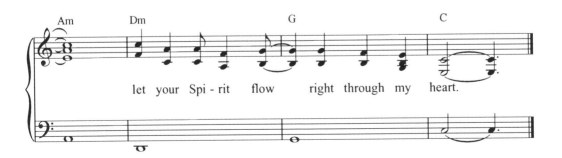

let your Spi - rit flow   right through my   heart.

37 I'm singing your praise, Lord

Words and Music: Mike Burn

2. I'm clapping my hands . . .

3. I'm shouting your name . . .

4. I'm jumping for joy . . .

38 I'm so excited

Words and Music: Audrey Traynor

1. I'm so ex - ci - ted, Lord, I can't keep still; I've got to
2. Just be - ing here with you is oh so pre - cious, it's a

jump up and down on my feet. 'Cos when I think a - bout the
feel - ing I will ne - ver for - get. And now I feel your Spi - rit

way that you love me, Lord, I know I can't just sit in my seat,
mov - ing with - in me, Lord, I thank you for this mo - ment we share,

no, ooh, it starts in my heart now,
yeah,

39 I'm special

Words and Music: Graham Kendrick

I'm spe-cial be-cause God has loved me, for he

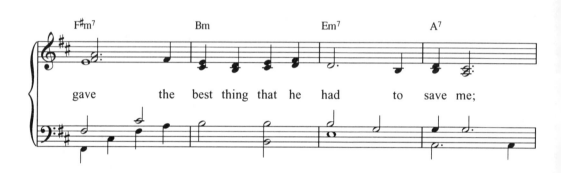

gave the best thing that he had to save me;

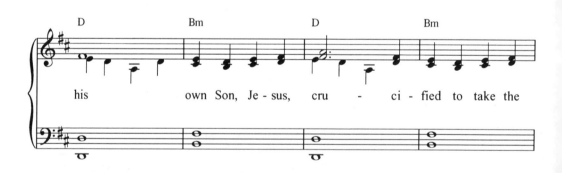

his own Son, Je-sus, cru - ci - fied to take the

blame, for all the bad things I have done.

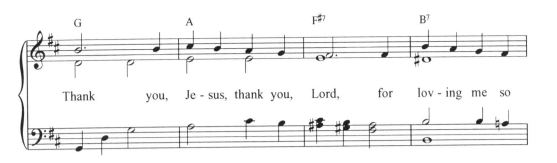

Thank you, Je - sus, thank you, Lord, for lov - ing me so

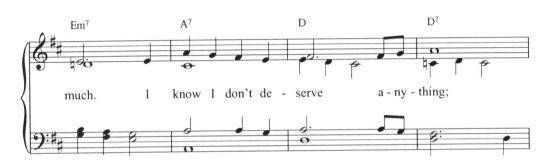

much. I know I don't de - serve a - ny - thing;

help me feel your love right now to know deep in my

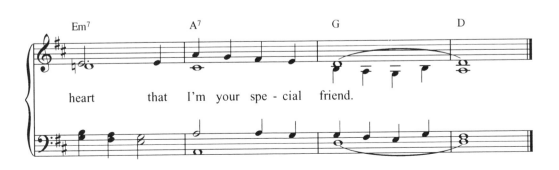

heart that I'm your spe - cial friend.

40 I never want anything   *(Heart and soul)*

Words and Music: Wes Sutton

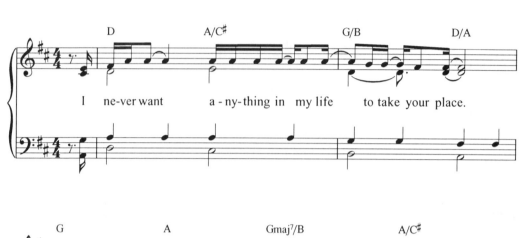

I ne-ver want a-ny-thing in my life to take your place.

I ne-ver want to live by a-ny o-ther grace. My

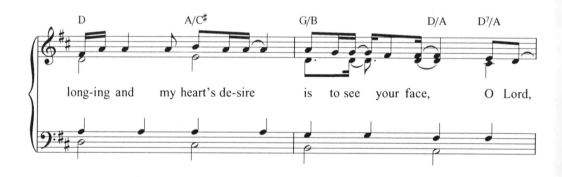

long-ing and my heart's de-sire is to see your face, O Lord,

and be-come a friend of God. I love you day and night,

I love you,   all my life,   I love you,   Lord,

heart and soul,   I long to be   a friend of God.

Family Worship

41 In Matthew, twenty-six   *(Watch and pray)*

Words and Music: Mike Burn

In Mat-thew, twen-ty-six, verse for-ty-one, Je-sus spoke these words to his friends: 'Watch and pray, watch and pray, so that you won't fall in-to temp-ta-tion. Watch and pray, watch and pray, the Spi-rit is will-ing but the bo-dy is weak.'

42 In the Spirit I rise

Words and Music: Judy Bailey

In the Spi-rit I rise, rise, I rise to your call,

in the Spi-rit I rise, rise, I rise up to your call.

In the Spi-rit I rise, rise, I rise to your call,

in the Spi-rit I rise, rise, I rise up to your call.

1. I have put my trust in God; Fa - ther, Spi - rit,

Son. When he calls me to come then I know I must res-pond, I

rise in the Spi - rit of love.

2. When things seem too hard for me
   I will not give up.
   You're the strength that I need,
   power when the flesh is weak,
   I rise in the Spirit of love.

3. I will live for you, my Lord,
   my future's in your hand.
   Here's my life for your plan,
   take me, Jesus, here I am,
   I rise in the Spirit of love.

43 I reach up high

Words and Music: Judy Bailey

I reach up high, I touch the ground, I stomp my feet and I turn a-round. I've got to (woo woo) praise the Lord.

I jump and dance with all my might, I might look fun-ny but that's al-right. I've got to (woo woo) praise the Lord.

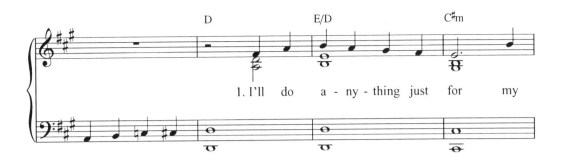

1. I'll do a - ny - thing just for my

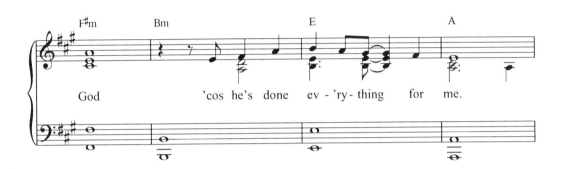

God 'cos he's done ev - 'ry - thing for me.

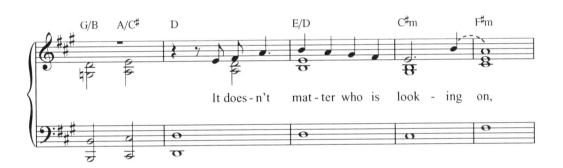

It does - n't mat - ter who is look - ing on,

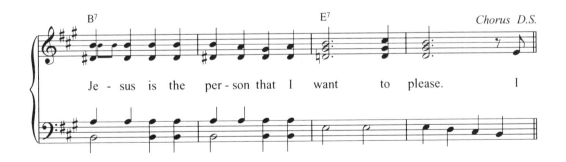

Je - sus is the per - son that I want to please. I

2. May my whole life be a song of praise
   to worship God in ev'ry way.
   In this song the actions praise his name,
   I want my actions ev'ry day to do the same.

44 Is anyone in trouble

Words and Music: Mike Burn

Is a-ny-one in trou-ble, they should pray; is a-ny-one hap-py, let them

sing songs of praise. Is sing songs of praise. Is

Is

a - ny - one sick? Let them call for the el - ders and the

prayer of faith will make the sick per - son well. Is sick per - son well.

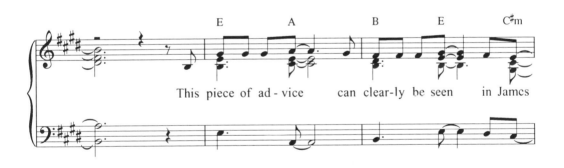

This piece of ad - vice can clear-ly be seen in James

chap - ter five, thir - teen to fif - teen.

45 I will lift up the name of the Lord

Words and Music: Mike Burn

46 I will proclaim

(All you've done)

Words and Music: Mike Burn

I will pro - claim your great - ness, my God and King,

I'll bless your name for e - ver and e - ver - more.

For you are great, your name to be high - ly praised,

my song shall be 'Great is the Lord.'

All you've done shall be praised to the com-ing ge-ne -

ra - tions; God, we shall de - clare your migh-ty deeds.

Men shall speak of your power, of your good-ness and your

mer - cy, that the child - ren may know,

To verses 2 and 3 | *Last time*

great is the Lord. 2. All of your

2. All of your works
   shall praise you, Creator God,
   and all the saints
   for ever will bless your name.
   O, they shall speak
   of glory and of royal pow'r.
   Their song shall be
   'Great is the Lord.'

3. O, righteous God,
   so gracious in all your ways,
   you rescue those
   who call out upon your name.
   You hear their cry
   and surely salvation comes.
   Their song shall be
   'Great is the Lord.'

47 Jesus Christ, you are the Son of God

(On my knees)

Words and Music: Andy Pressdee and Ian Mizen
arr. Richard Lewis

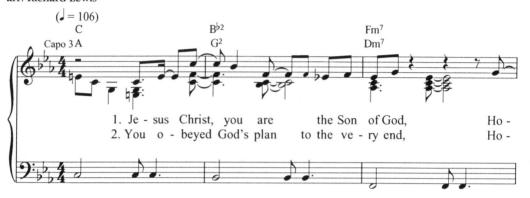

1. Je - sus Christ, you are the Son of God, Ho -
2. You o - beyed God's plan to the ve - ry end, Ho -

- ly One, you gave ev - 'ry - thing to be - come
- ly One, be - came the sac - ri - fice that would show

like one of us. Hea - ven's Son
us the Fa - ther's love. You came to die

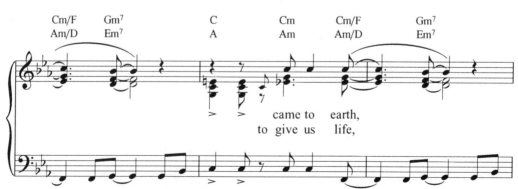

came to earth,
to give us life,

One day all the world will see you, one day all the world will see all cre - a - tion kneel be - fore you, all cre - a - tion sing.

Family Worship

48 Jesus' love has got under our skin

(Under our skin)

Words and Music: Graham Kendrick

Je-sus' love has got un-der our skin, Je-sus'

love has got un-der our skin. Je - sus'

Deep-er than col - our oh; rich-er than

cul - ture oh; strong-er than e - mo - tion oh;

wid-er than the o - cean oh. Don't you want to

49 Jesus loves me

Words: Jenny Legg

Music: Tim Oliver and Jenny Legg

2. Jesus loves the little sheep,
   the Good Shepherd, he will keep
   watching over ev'ryone:
   when he calls, I will come.

3. As I close my eyes to rest,
   I know I will do my best:
   I will follow, I will pray,
   I will walk in his way.

50 Jesus, name that we adore (This land)

Words and Music: Jo Puleston

2. And in your mercy, change our hearts
   to pray in the lost.
   Take our lives and fan the flame
   of passion for your name.

51 Jesus, thank you for the cross

Words and Music: Mike Burn

Je-sus, thank you for the cross, hold-ing no-thing back, you did all your Fa - ther asked. I'll ne-ver know just how it felt as you died, lift - ed high. I know it hurt, I know the pain was more than words could e - ver say.

Family Worship

52 Jesus, you're the morning star

Words: Mike Burn

Music: Traditional

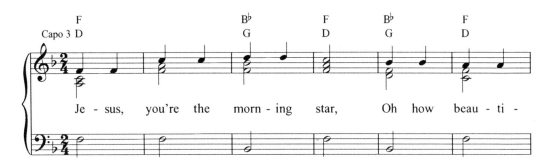

Je - sus, you're the morn - ing star, Oh how beau - ti -

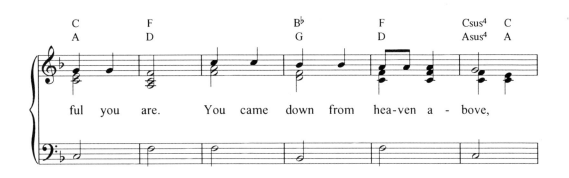

ful you are. You came down from hea-ven a - bove,

died to show the Fa - ther's love. Je - sus, you're the

morn - ing star, Oh how beau - ti - ful you are.

53 Let praise break out

Words and Music: Mike Burn

Let praise break out and let wor - ship flow, God's

name be praised and his glo - ry known. Let glo - ry known.

Build up, build up the high - way; raise a ban - ner for the

na - tions. Right - eous - ness, right - eous - ness and

praise   shall spring up be - fore   all na-tions.   See your

Sa - viour come, see your Sa - viour come, so let praise   break

out   and let   wor - ship   flow.

54 Let's get fit

Words and Music: Kath Fathers

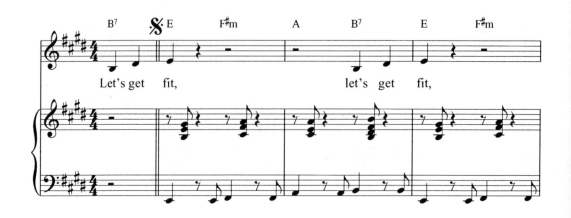

Let's get fit, let's get fit,

let's get fit, let's get fit. It's

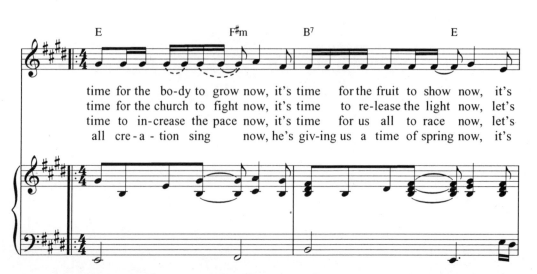

time for the bo-dy to grow now, it's time   for the fruit to show now, it's
time for the church to fight now, it's time   to re-lease the light now, let's
time to in-crease the pace now, it's time   for us all to race now, let's
all cre-a-tion sing   now, he's giv-ing us a time of spring now, it's

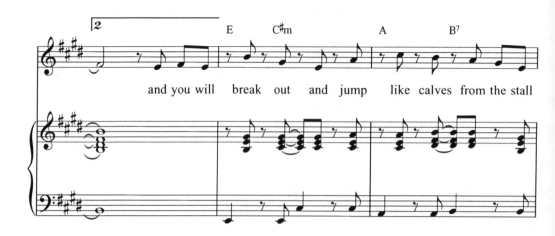

and you will break out and jump like calves from the stall

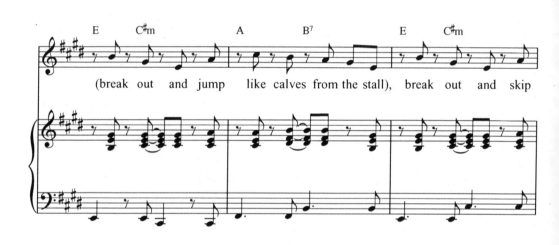

(break out and jump like calves from the stall), break out and skip

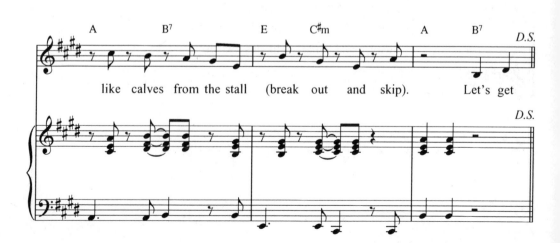

like calves from the stall (break out and skip). Let's get

Family Worship

55 Let us run

Words and Music: David Lyle Morris

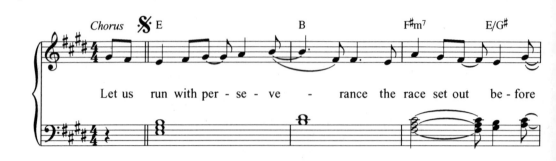

Chorus

Let us run with per - se - ve - rance the race set out be - fore

us, let us fix our eyes on Je - sus, the

au - thor and per - fec - tor of our faith.

1. In the be - gin - ning the word was with God, through him

all of us were made.

He be-gan a work in us, a good work to per-fect un-til

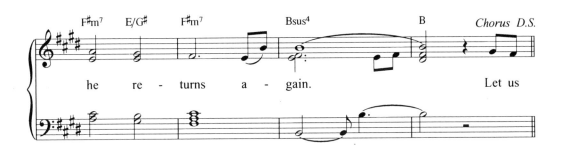

he re - turns a - gain. Let us

2. Since we are surrounded by heaven's cheering crowd,
   let us throw off ev'ry chain.
   For all that opposes us look to Jesus who endured,
   so we'll not lose heart again.

3. For the joy before him, he suffered the cross,
   he defeated death and shame.
   Now he reigns in glory at the right hand of God,
   he is calling us by name.

56 Lord, help me to tell your story

Words and Music: Tim Moyler and Donna Vann

1. Lord, help me to tell your sto - ry   to those who've ne - ver heard,
   help me to tell your sto - ry   of what you've done for me.
   so ma - ny live in dark - ness,   lost in an end - less night.

how you lived and died for us;   you are
Give me cour - age, Lord, to say   how you
Help them search and find you, Lord,   and fill

the way   to God.
have set   me free.
them with   your light.   I want to go,

Lord, in your pow - er, tell - ing the sto - ry of your name.

Family Worship

57 Lord, I love your name   *(Lift high the name)*

Words and Music: Mike Burn

1. Lord, I love your name, it's the great-est name I know, it's the name of peace, the name of heal-ing, from your name sal - va-tion flows.

I ex - alt your name, and my voice with joy I'll raise, from now un - til e - ter - ni-ty with songs and shouts of praise.

Chorus
Lift high the name, the name of Je-sus, for he is

great and wor-thy of praise. Glo - ri-ous, vic - to - ri-ous;

awe-some in his power. With ev-'ry breath, with all that's with-

in me; I'll lift his name high o - ver all,

Je - sus, Je - sus, Je - sus is Lord.

2. Lord, reveal your name,
let the world now stand in awe.
May your glory shine
throughout the nations,
praise resound from shore to shore.
Jesus, you're the Lamb,
you now sit upon the throne.
All power and authority
belong to you alone.

58 Lord, our Master

Words and Music: Dave Godfrey

With a reggae feel

Lord, our Mas-ter, won-der-ful is your name.

O Lord, our Mas-ter,

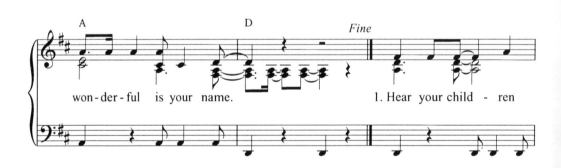

won-der-ful is your name. 1. Hear your child - ren

sing - ing prai - ses to the King, e - ne-mies are

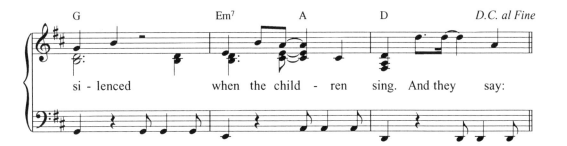

si - lenced   when the child - ren   sing. And they   say:

2. I gaze into the heavens,
   when the sunlight fades:
   moon and stars are gleaming,
   so beautifully made.
   And I say . . .

3. Why are we so special,
   you care for ev'ryone,
   you've crowned us with the glory
   of the risen Son.
   And we say . . .

4. You've given us control
   of animals like sheep;
   of birds and fish and creatures
   that live within the deep.
   And we say . . .

5. For all your might wonders
   and ev'ry thing we do,
   we will lift our voices
   and sing this song to you.
   And we say . . .

59 Lord, we cry out

Words and Music: Ken McGreavy and Wes Sutton

2. Open our eyes to see.
   Open our eyes to see.
   We want to see,
   we want to see you.

3. Lord, we will follow you.
   Lord, we will follow you.
   We'll follow you,
   we'll follow in the way of truth.

60 Lord, we lift you high

Words and Music: Judy Bailey

61 Lost in adoration

(All heaven sings)

Words and Music: Dave Bankhead and John Gibson

1. Lost in a-do-ra - tion, our voi - ces we raise,

with the host of hea - ven, lift you to the high - est place,

mul - ti - tudes in awe be - fore the glo - ry of your throne; our

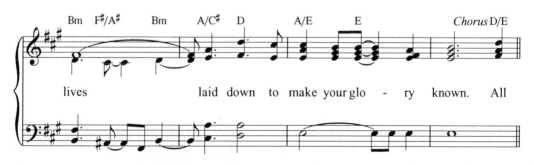

lives laid down to make your glo - ry known. All

heav-en's voi - ces ring, ten thou-sand an - gels sing; 'All hail to Je - sus our King!' Let ev - 'ry na - tion sing, their a - do - ra - tion ring-ing out; 'All hail to Je - sus our King!'

2. Ev'ry tribe and nation
shall honour your name;
see your great salvation
on the day you come to reign.
Focus of our adoration
may our lives convey;
we long to see
the dawning of your day.

62 Love, joy, peace   *(The fruit of the Spirit)*

Words and Music: David Lyle Morris

C	C/E	D	G	C⁶	D⁷

we will re-joice in the Spi-rit of God.

G	G	G/B	C/D	G

There is   peace   in the Spi - rit,

C	C/E	D	G	C⁶	D⁷	G	D.C.

we want to rest in the Spi-rit of God.

G	G/B	C⁶	D

Walk - ing with the Spi - rit of Je -
Liv - ing by the Spi - rit of Je -
Re-joic - ing in the Spi - rit of Je -
Rest - ing in the Spi - rit of Je -

G	G/B	C⁶	D⁶	Repeat x4	G

- sus.
- sus.
- sus.
- sus.

2. We want life in the Spirit,
   we want to live by the Spirit of God,
   keep in step with the Spirit,
   we will be led by the Spirit of God.

63 My soul thirsts for you

(Waterfall)

Words and Music: Ian Mizen, Andy Pressdee
and Kath Fathers

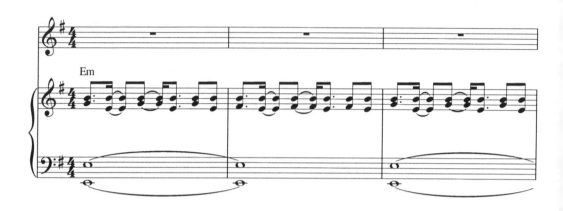

1. My soul   thirsts for you,   my soul
2. I need   more of you,   I need

thirsts   for   you   like a dry land,
more   of   you.   Fill me, Lord,

Family Worship

64 No one ever spoke   *(There is only one Jesus)*

Words and Music: Graeme Young

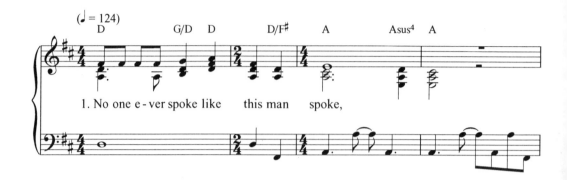

1. No one e-ver spoke like this man spoke,

gen-tle words with life - giv-ing power.

No one e - ver did like this man did,

chal-lenged e - vil, mak-ing it flee.

Chorus

There is, there is on - ly, there is on - ly one Je - sus,

there is, there is on - ly, there is on - ly one Je - sus.

2. No one ever loved like this man loved,
   glad to be friend to the despised.
   No one ever healed like this man healed,
   blind eyes saw the lame jump for joy.

3. No one ever lived like this man lived,
   heaven touched the earth where he walked.
   No one ever felt like this man felt,
   carrying the pain of the world.

4. No one ever died like this man died,
   saying it was God's love for us.
   No one ever rose like this man rose,
   shown in pow'r to be Son of God.

65 Nothing is impossible for God

Words and Music: Jane M. Young (written when aged 12)

2. There's a battle going on and the ending's known,
   when Jesus as our King will take his place.
   We fight for love, for happiness and peace,
   we fight that others may see us with his face.

3. Thank you, Lord, for loving me so much,
   for giving me a place deep in your heart,
   for holding me in your protecting arms,
   for forgiving and understanding from the start.

Family Worship

66 Oh, don't worry

Words and Music: Mike Burn

67 Oh, I'm fighting

Words and Music: Mike Burn

Oh, I'm fight-ing, but not a-gainst peo-ple,

it's a bat-tle of good and e-vil.

But I don't need a gun, I don't need a sword, I don't need

sticks and I don't need stones, my wea-pons are not of this

world. I'll fight with a prayer of faith, I'll fight with a

68 O, King of love

Words and Music: Jo Puleston

free. Wor - ship, Je - sus,

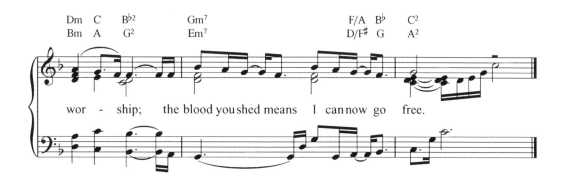

wor - ship; the blood you shed means I can now go free.

69 Our Father in heaven   *(The Lord's Prayer)*

Words and Music: Dave Bankhead and Mike Burn

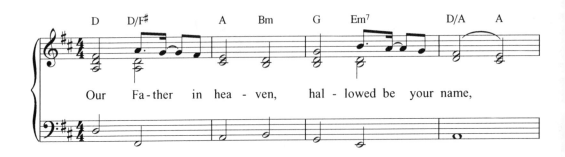

Our Fa-ther in hea-ven, hal-lowed be your name,

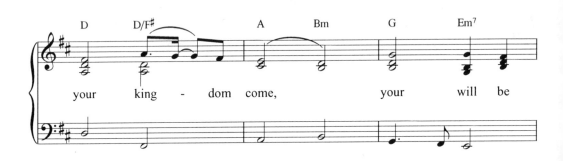

your king - dom come, your will be

done on earth as it is in hea-ven;

give us to-day our dai - ly bread, and for-give us our

sins as we for - give those who sin a - gainst us.

Lead us not in - to temp - ta - tion, but de - li - ver us from

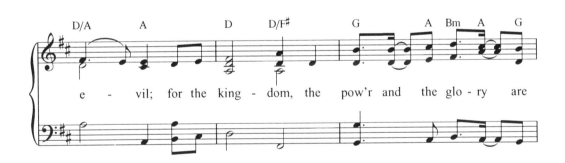

e - vil; for the king - dom, the pow'r and the glo - ry are

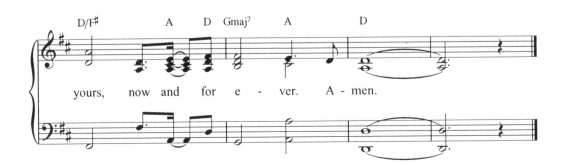

yours, now and for e - ver. A - men.

70 Pass it on

Words and Music: Mike Burn

Pass it on, God is so

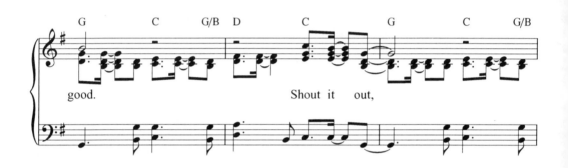

good. Shout it out,

Je - sus is Lord. The

church of God is a - ris - ing, his Spi - rit is mov - ing us

out,   we're march-ing   with love as   our ban-ner,   we're

rais-ing   a vic-to-ry shout.   With one voice we'll sing,   with

one voice we'll cry,   Je-sus   is Lord,   we'll   lift his name

high.   Pass it   on,   Pass it   on.

71 Pray at all times

Words and Music: Mike Burn

Pray at all times, ne - ver ceas - ing,

ask for what you need with thanks - giv - ing.

Join to - ge - ther in a - gree - ment

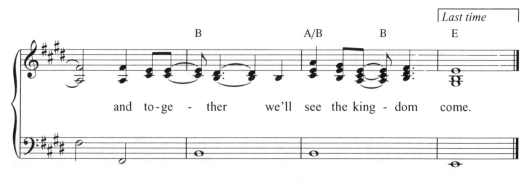

and to - ge - ther we'll see the king - dom come.

To continue

come. Give thanks to the Fa - ther for he

hears all our prayers, give thanks to the Son for he

prays for us, give thanks to the Spi - rit for when we don't

know how to pray; he will plead with

God on our be - half. Pray at all

72 Prayer can make a difference

Words and Music: Mike Burn

Chorus

Prayer can make a dif - f'rence, prayer can make a dif - f'rence,

prayer can make a dif - f'rence, so pray!

Prayer can make a dif - f'rence, prayer can make a dif - f'rence,

To verse 2 / Last time *To verse 1*

prayer can make a dif - f'rence, so pray! pray! 1. Through

prayer, our God can heal. We be - lieve in mi - ra -

73 See the love of God poured out

(Look to the cross)

Words and Music: Mike Burn

See the love of God poured out, look to the cross,

gaze up-on the one we pierced, look to the cross.

See him taste the bit-ter wine, look to the cross,

'It is fin-ished' was his cry, look to the cross.

Chorus

Look to the cross, there the King of Love was

lift-ed up   for all the world to see.   Look to the blood

flow-ing from his side,   it's pow'r re-leased for all e-ter-ni-ty.

On-ly   one man,   on-ly   one God could lay down his life   for

me,   Je   -   sus.

2. Know your sin that caused his pain,
    kneel at the cross,
    ask forgiveness in his name,
    kneel at the cross.
    Wonder at the price he paid,
    kneel at the cross,
    all your guilt is washed away,
    kneel at the cross.

3. Die to self to rise with him,
    share in the cross,
    glory's won through suffering,
    share in the cross.
    Joy before him, Christ endured,
    share in the cross,
    lives redeemed his great reward,
    share in the cross.

74 Some days are not easy *(Trust in the Lord)*

Words and Music: Tim Moyler
and the Ichthus Beckenham children

Some days are not ea-sy, some days are tough.

Some-times peo-ple hurt you and you've just had e-nough.

Where have all your friends gone, who can you find to

lis-ten to the wor-ries that spin round in your mind?

Tell me what shall I do, who can I trust?

75 Spirit, Holy Spirit

Words and Music: Judy Bailey

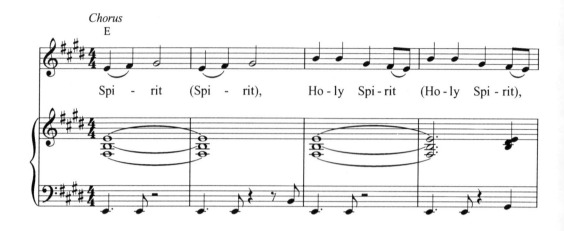

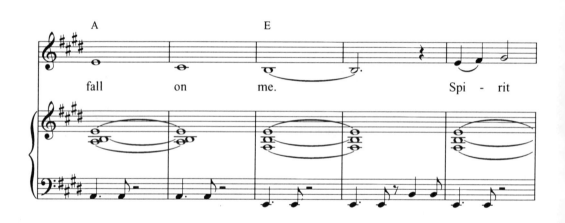

Family Worship

76 Thank you, heavenly Father *(Jesus in my house)*

Words and Music: Judy Bailey

Thank you, heav'n-ly Fa-ther, for your love for me,

I'm for e-ver grate-ful that you sac-ri-ficed your Son.

You saved my soul and changed my des-ti-ny,

thank you, God, for Je-sus in me. I'm so glad that

Je - sus lives   in my house,   good to know that he   is here   with me now,

all of my life,   Je - sus in me,   Je - sus in my

house.   All of my life,   and al - ways will be.

2. Thank you for the purpose you have placed in me,
   thank you for forgiveness and the chance to start again.
   I face the future knowing I will be
   safe and sound with Jesus in me.

77 The depth of a mystery (Communion song)

Words and Music: Mike Burn

Family Worship

78 The fear of the Lord

Words and Music: Mike Burn

per - fect love cast out all o - ther fear. Come be - fore him with

rev -'rence, as a ho - ly God he is sure - ly to be feared.

Family Worship

79 The heavens are open *(We're praying)*

Words and Music: Jo Puleston
arr. Dave Bankhead

* *Echos are optional*

80 The Lord is gracious

Words and Music: Jo Puleston

The Lord is gra-cious and com-pas - sion-ate,

slow to an - ger, rich in love,

the Lord is good to all who call on him,

to all who call on him in truth, so I

lift my eyes in des-pe-ra-tion, my on-ly hope to see this through. I

can't go on one step with-out you, your faith-ful-ness I know is

true.

81 There is a place *(No one loves me like Jesus)*

Words and Music: Kath Fathers

1. There is a place where I can go
2. There is a se - cret place to go

when I'm feel-ing lone - ly or a-fraid; there is a
where some-bo - dy knows me ve - ry well; there is a

place where I can go that is spe-cial to me.
se - cret place to go where I can be me.

There is a love that's kind and warm, a love that will kiss
And there my lov - ing Je - sus smiles, he o - pens his arms

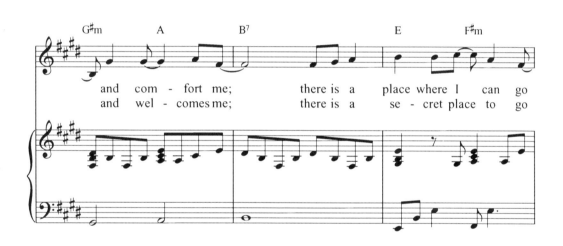

and com - fort me; there is a place where I can go
and wel - comes me; there is a se - cret place to go

that is spe-cial to me.
where I can be me.

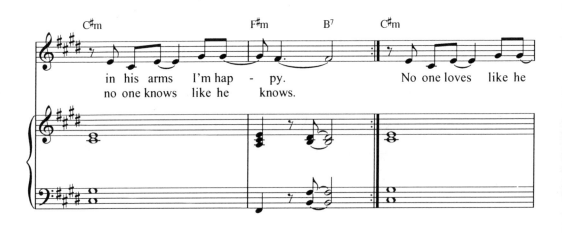

Family Worship

82 Through the cross
(Healing river)

Words and Music: Mike Burn

Through the cross, Je-sus, you tri-umphed, by your

blood you bought our peace. Where there once was death and se-pa-

ra-tion, your heal-ing ri-ver flows. Let it

flow, let it flow, let the heal - ing ri-ver flow. Gra-cious

God, we cry to you, let the heal-ing ri - ver flow.

To verses | *Last time*

2. Bind up

2. Bind up wounds within our homes, Lord,
   reconcile husbands and wives.
   Turn the fathers' hearts towards their children,
   oh, let the river flow.

3. Break down walls of isolation,
   rescue those who live in fear.
   May the lonely find love in your fam'ly,
   oh, let the river flow.

4. May your church rise up as one now,
   join the streams in one accord.
   Young and old will stand and sing with one voice,
   to praise our risen Lord.

83 To be in your presence, Lord

Words and Music: Mike Burn

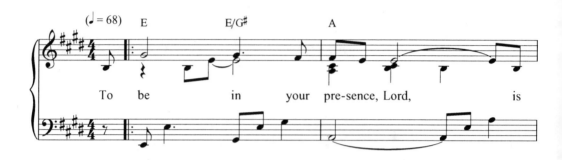

To be in your pre-sence, Lord, is

more than life to me. Sur - round - ed by your

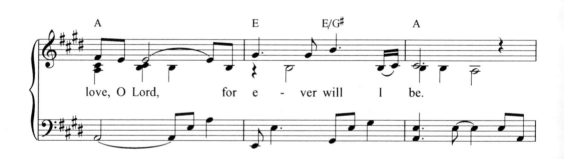

love, O Lord, for e - ver will I be.

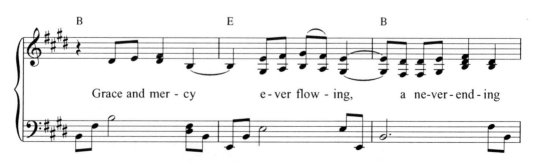

Grace and mer - cy e - ver flow - ing, a ne-ver-end-ing

stream.   Draw me now in - to your pre - sence, Lord,

as   I   draw near   to   you,   my   Lord.

To

84 To know your love
(To know you)

Words and Music: Ian Mizen and Andy Pressdee

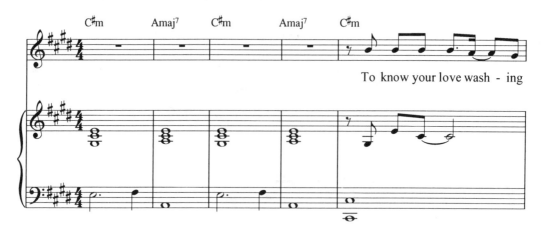

To know your love wash - ing

o - ver me,   your sweet for - give-ness cov - 'ring me,

to know your heart and mind   and hear your voice call - ing

With all my heart, my soul, my strength,   I

wor-ship you   with all my heart, my soul, my strength,

I   love   you.   I   love   you.

Family Worship

85 To obey is better than sacrifice

Words and Music: Mike Burn

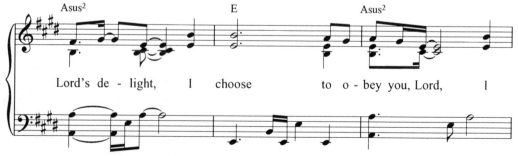

choose   to lay down my   life,   not my will but yours be

done,   in my life,   may   your king - dom come.

86 To the cross I come

Words and Music: Jo Puleston

2. To the cross I come, and kneel upon this ground
   where streams of mercy flow.
   To the cross I come, and lay my burdens down
   as love restores my soul.

3. To the cross I come, here to worship you
   and thank you for my life.
   To the cross I come, here to worship you,
   precious Holy Lamb.

87 We are God's chosen holy nation

(Rising generation)

Words and Music: Dave Bankhead and Mike Burn

We are God's cho- sen ho-ly na- tion, we be-

long to him a-lone and may this ris - ing ge-ne-ra-

-tion wor-ship Christ up-on his throne, wor-ship

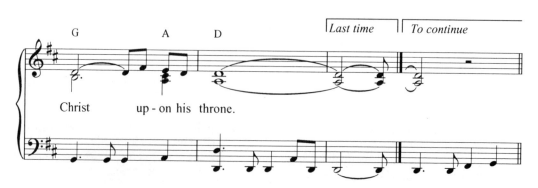

Christ up-on his throne.

1. We be-lieve in God the Fa - ther, and in Christ, his pre-cious

Son. We be-lieve he died to save us,

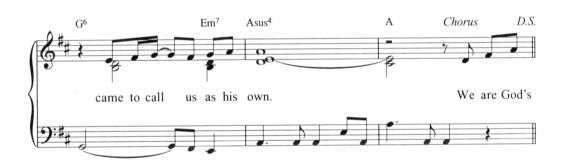

came to call us as his own. *Chorus* We are God's

2. We believe he sends his Spirit
on us now with gifts of power.
Hear the Spirit calling out to us
where he leads us we will go.

88 We'll stand up and fight   *(Stand up and fight)*

Words and Music: Dave Bankhead and Steve Bassett

1. We'll stand up and fight for jus-tice and free-dom, we'll burn with a light that shines like the Son. One hope and one faith, one Lord and one vis-ion, one prayer for this world that his king-dom shall come.

2. We stand in his sight,
   a people forgiven.
   Our love shining bright
   like a light to the world.
   Our pray'r for his church,
   Lord, heal our divisions
   for we work within sight
   of a new day to come.

89 We must work together

(We'll see it all)

Words and Music: Ian Mizen and Andy Pressdee

1. We must work to-ge-ther, bring-ing in the king-dom, bring-ing hea-ven here on earth. Start a new world or-der, start a re-vo-lu-tion, let all peo-ple know their worth.

2. We will see the dawn-ing, in this ge-ne-ra-tion see the start of a new day. We'll know peace and free-dom, we will know true laugh-ter, we'll see sick-ness blown a-way.

Chorus

Call We'll see it all, *Response* we'll see it all, *Call* we'll see it all,

90 We stand united

(We are all one)

Words and Music: Dave Bankhead

We stand u-ni-ted in a love bought by his blood, one ho-ly na-tion and one ri-sen Lord, and joined to-ge-ther o-ver-seas from shore to shore we shall lift the name of Je-sus high once more. We are all one,

Chorus

joined by the Spi-rit a-gain, we are all

2. Just as the Father stands united with the Son,
   though we are many, he has made us one.
   In ev'ry nation, that the world at last might see
   we will shout aloud that Jesus sets men free!

91 We've got to see an end *(Waiting for the healing)*

Words and Music: Ian Mizen and Andy Pressdee

1. We've got to see an end to the pain, the tears and the hurt - ing. How long must we wait for you to move and bring an end to suf - fer - ing?

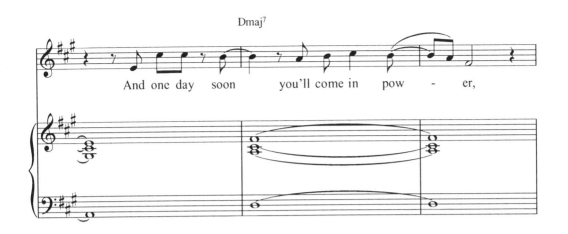

Dmaj[7]

And one day soon you'll come in pow - er,

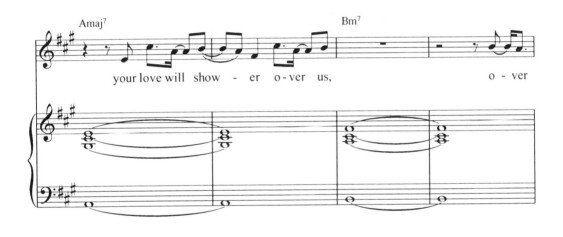

Amaj[7]   Bm[7]

your love will show - er o - ver us,   o - ver

1.   2.

F♯m   F♯m

us.   We're wait-ing   for the   us.

92 We will turn the hearts

Words and Music: Kath Fathers

looking to Je - sus to car - ry us through. All diff-'rent ra - ces,

all diff-'rent a - ges, all of us here of your glo - ry. And we

call on your Spi - rit, keep us to- ge - ther and pour in your power. We will

2. The walls have been broken, we stand as one now,
   one in the Spirit and won by your blood.
   We're moving forwards under your banner,
   telling the world of your glory
   and we take on your promise;
   together we'll welcome the day of the Lord!

93 When you pray

Words and Music: Mike Burn

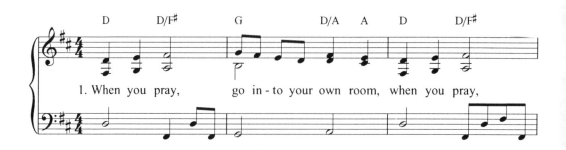

1. When you pray, go in-to your own room, when you pray,

close the door. When you pray, go in-to your own room,

when you pray, close the door. Pray to Fa - ther, who

is un-seen, and your Fa - ther, who sees what you do; he'll re-ward

94 Whiter than the snow

Words and Music: Mike Burn

95 Who could have dared to dream it? *(Peace Child)*

Words and Music: Mike Burn

1. Who could have dared to dream it, who would have dared to hope? That the Au - thor of cre - a - tion should be-come as one of us. The God who is ev - 'ry-where chose to be con - fined to a mo - ment in his - to - ry; the birth of a child. And an o - cean of love poured out, a

New Year, we give thanks for the past for we know our God is faith - ful, he is wor-thy of our trust. And through the world's suf - fer - ing, through all the pain, he knows what it feels like, he knew it as a man. And an o - cean of love poured out, a

Family Worship

96 You accept me as I am

(Perfect love)

Words and Music: Mike Burn

1. You ac - cept me as I am, you love me through and
   nei - ther death nor life nor an - gels, rul - ers,
   cleanse me by your blood and lead me in - to

through; Lord, where can I go to flee your
pow - ers, nor things that are, nor things that are to
free - dom; for per - fect love casts out the fear with -

pre - sence? No sin can se - pa - rate,
come. Not a - ny height or depth,
in me. Re - veal your Fa - ther heart

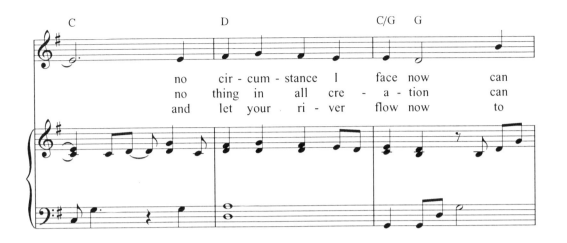

no cir-cum-stance I face now can
no thing in all cre-a-tion can
and let your ri-ver flow now to

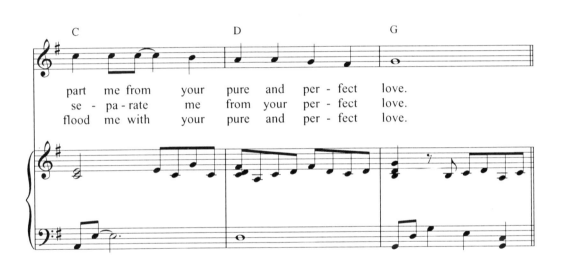

part me from your pure and per-fect love.
se-pa-rate me from your per-fect love.
flood me with your pure and per-fect love.

Chorus

flows from the Fa - ther, flows through the

Per-fect love, per - fect love.

97 You are a kind and loving God
(You did not leave us)

Words and Music: Judy Bailey

You are a kind and lov - ing God, you keep us safe; watch o - ver us. You know our lives in ev - 'ry part, you care for us. You did not leave us on the earth all a - lone and out of touch, but you left

your home in hea - ven; gave your life up - on the cross. We are guid-

- ed by your Spi - rit, we are fa - thered by your love, you care

for us, you care for us.

2. Your ways are true, your ways are just,
   you dry our tears when times are tough.
   You're strong when we're not strong enough,
   you care for us.

3. Unshaken in your faithfulness,
   you hear our prayers and answer them.
   You discipline the ones you love,
   you care for us.

98 You are the best

Words and Music: Tim Moyler
and the children of Ichthus Beckenham

You are the best, bet-ter than all the rest,

Je-sus, you're the best. You are the best, bet-ter than all the rest,

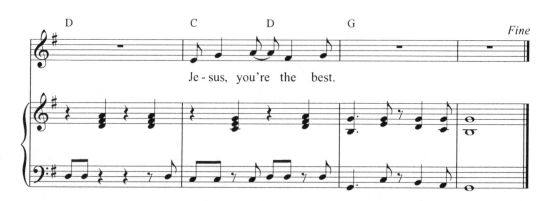

Je-sus, you're the best.

1. Je-sus, we love you be-cause you died up-on the cross.

Thank you, Lord, for dy - ing for our sins.

To verses 2 & 4

You are the best,

2. When we feel that life is like a storm
   you give your peace.
   When we need you
   Lord, you rescue us.

3. Thank you, Lord, for giving us
   our food and drink each day.
   When we're sick
   you heal us with your love.

4. Lord, we love to praise you
   for you love and care for us.
   We want to get to know you
   more each day.

99 You put a new song in my mouth

Words and Music: Mark Harris

2. Many will see what the Lord had done,
   they'll be amazed and trust in you.
   Blessed are those who trust you, Lord,
   all you do is marvellous.
   So much to tell,
   your plans for us are wonderful.

100 Your name is wonderful

(Glory)

Words and Music: Jo Puleston

Keyword Index

Scriptural Index

Index of First Lines

This index gives the first line of each song.
If a song is known by an alternative title, this is also given, but indented and in italics.

Albums and websites where song recordings may be found

First Line and Song Title	Album	Website
All the world can offer *(Because)*	world wide worship	kevinmayhewltd.com
A rainfall in drought *(By your wounds)*	Not available	
A time to mourn and a time to dance	FW2 - With One Voice	familyworship.org.uk
Be joyful	Teach us to pray	familyworship.org.uk
Calling on the Spirit	FW3 - Fire and Rain	familyworship.org.uk
Celebrate Jesus	Celebrez L'Eternel	ian.booth.free.fr/home
Christ before me	FW4 - Rising Generation	familyworship.org.uk
Come and sing	FW2 - With One Voice	familyworship.org.uk
Crossing over	FW1 - Let Praise Break Out	familyworship.org.uk
Drawn from every tribe *(Revelation 7)*	Not available	davidlylemorris.com
Everywhere I go *(Jesus my friend)*	Not available	
Father, I do adore you	FW1 - Let Praise Break Out	familyworship.org.uk
Father's seeking those who'll worship *(With one voice)*	FW2 - With One Voice	familyworship.org.uk
Fill my life O Lord my God *(Praying God)*	Not available	judybailey.com
Fly free *(Song for Wales)*	FW4 - Rising Generation	familyworship.org.uk
From where the sun rises	No More Walls	makewaymusic.com
Give, and it shall be given	FW4 - Rising Generation	familyworship.org.uk
God is our Father	When the music fades	davidlylemorris.com
God, you can use me	FW1 - Let Praise Break Out	familyworship.org.uk
Grace and love	Not available	
Have you not seen? *(Fire and Rain)*	FW3 - Fire and Rain	familyworship.org.uk
Heavenly Father *(Prayer Song)*	Amazed	brownbearmusic.co.uk
Here I'm bowed	Not available	
Holy Jesus	To Know You	brownbearmusic.co.uk
Hosanna	Celebrez L'Eternel	ian.booth.free.fr/home
I'd reach for the stars	FW3 - Fire and Rain	familyworship.org.uk
I exalt your name	Not available	
If I look in a mirror	Not available	familyworship.org.uk
If we admit to God	FW1 - Let Praise Break Out	familyworship.org.uk
If we were to keep quiet	FW1 - Let Praise Break Out	familyworship.org.uk
If you believe	Teach us to pray	familyworship.org.uk
If you have faith	Not available	familyworship.org.uk
I love to be with you, Jesus *(To be with you)*	FW3 - Fire and Rain	familyworship.org.uk
I'm gonna dance on the streets *(Dance on the streets)*	FW3 - Fire and Rain	familyworship.org.uk
I'm putting God's armour on	Not available	familyworship.org.uk
I'm putting my hand in your hand	FW1 - Let Praise Break Out	familyworship.org.uk
I'm singing your praise, Lord	FW1 - Let Praise Break Out	familyworship.org.uk
I'm so excited	FW3 - Fire and Rain	familyworship.org.uk
I'm special	Various	makewaymusic.com
I never want anything in my life *(Heart and soul)*	Not available	
In Matthew, twenty-six *(Watch and pray)*	Teach us to pray	familyworship.org.uk
In the Spirit I rise	FW4 - Rising Generation	familyworship.org.uk
I reach up high	FW1 - Let Praise Break Out	familyworship.org.uk
Is anyone in trouble	Teach us to pray	familyworship.org.uk
I will lift up the name of the Lord	FW4 - Rising Generation	familyworship.org.uk
I will proclaim *(All you've done)*	Not available	familyworship.org.uk
Jesus Christ, you are the Son of God *(On my knees)*	Not available	familyworship.org.uk

Song	Album	Website
Jesus love has got under our skin *(Under our skin)*	No More Walls	makewaymusic.com
Jesus loves me	Sing Lullabies	iccrecords.com
Jesus, name that we adore *(This land)*	Not available	mp3.com/jopuleston
Jesus, thank you for the cross	FW3 - Fire and Rain	familyworship.org.uk
Jesus, you're the morning star	Spring Harvest Little Kids	familyworship.org.uk
Let it rain, let it rain *(Love rain down)*	FW3 - Fire and Rain	familyworship.org.uk
Let praise break out	FW1 - Let Praise Break Out	familyworship.org.uk
Let's get fit	FW2 - With One Voice	familyworship.org.uk
Let us run	FW3 - Fire and Rain	familyworship.org.uk
Lord, help me to tell your story	FW4 - Rising Generation	familyworship.org.uk
Lord, I love your name *(Lift high the name)*	Not available	familyworship.org.uk
Lord our master	Heaven's No. 1	iccrecords.com
Lord we cry out to you	FW2 - With One Voice	familyworship.org.uk
Lord we lift you high	FW2 - With One Voice	familyworship.org.uk
Lost in adoration *(All heaven sings)*	All heaven sings	weareone.org.uk
Love, joy, peace *(The fruit of the Spirit)*	King of the Ages	davidlylemorris.com
My soul thirsts for you *(Waterfall)*	FW2 - With One Voice	familyworship.org.uk
No one ever spoke *(There is only one Jesus)*	Not available	youngresources.co.uk
Nothing is impossible for God	Not available	youngresources.co.uk
O God, you are my God *(Better than life)*	FW4 - Rising Generation	familyworship.org.uk
Oh don't worry	Teach us to pray	familyworship.org.uk
Oh, I'm fighting	Teach us to pray	familyworship.org.uk
O King of love	FW4 - Rising Generation	familyworship.org.uk
Our Father in heaven *(The Lord's Prayer)*	Teach us to pray	familyworship.org.uk
Pass it on	Not available	familyworship.org.uk
Pray at all times	Teach us to pray	familyworship.org.uk
Prayer can make a difference	Teach us to pray	familyworship.org.uk
See the love of God poured out *(Look to the cross)*	Not available	familyworship.org.uk
Some days are not easy	FW3 - Fire and Rain	familyworship.org.uk
Spirit, Holy Spirit	FW2 - With One Voice	familyworship.org.uk
Thank you, heavenly Father *(Jesus in my house)*	Jesus in my house	judybailey.com
The depth of a mystery *(Communion Song)*	FW4 - Rising Generation	familyworship.org.uk
The fear of the Lord	Not available	familyworship.org.uk
The heavens are open	The heavens are open	mp3.com/jopuleston
The Lord is gracious	Not available	mp3.com/jopuleston
There is a place *(No-one loves me like Jesus)*	FW2 - With One Voice	familyworship.org.uk
Through the cross *(Healing river)*	FW3 - Fire and Rain	familyworship.org.uk
To be in your presence, Lord	Not available	familyworship.org.uk
To know your love *(To know you)*	To Know You	brownbearmusic.co.uk
To obey is better than sacrifice	Not available	familyworship.org.uk
To the cross I come	Not available	mp3.com/jopuleston
We are God's chosen holy nation *(Rising generation)*	FW4 - Rising Generation	familyworship.org.uk
We'll stand up and fight *(Stand up and fight)*	All heaven sings	weareone.org.uk
We must work together *(We'll see it all)*	My soul thirsts for you	brownbearmusic.co.uk
We stand united *(We are all one)*	We are one	weareone.org.uk
We've got to see an end *(Waiting for the healing)*	Amazed	brownbearmusic.co.uk
We will turn the hearts	FW1 - Let Praise Break Out	familyworship.org.uk
When you pray	Teach us to pray	familyworship.org.uk
Whiter than the snow	FW4 - Rising Generation	familyworship.org.uk
Who could have dared to dream it? *(Peace Child)*	FW4 - Rising Generation	familyworship.org.uk
You accept me as I am *(Perfect Love)*	FW2 - With One Voice	familyworship.org.uk
You are a kind and loving God	FW3 - Fire and Rain	familyworship.org.uk
You are the best	FW2 - With One Voice	familyworship.org.uk